Beautiful America's

California Victorians

Front Cover: A montage of Victorian gables.

Published by
Beautiful America Publishing Company
PO Box 244
Woodburn, Oregon 97071

Design: Ancel Van Renes

Library of Congress Catalog Number 98-4295

ISBN 0-89802-701-2
ISBN 0-89802-700-4 (Paperback)

Printed in Korea

William Carson Mansion, Eureka, 1886

Beautiful America's
California Victorians

Text & Photography
by
Kenneth Naversen

Contents

Introduction

When General Mariano Vallejo ordered a prefabricated Gothic Revival cottage from Boston back in the gold rush era, he probably didn't realize he was starting an architectural trend. But he must have known he was getting a deal—a stylish new residence for his estate in Sonoma at a time when many people in California were sleeping in tents. In any event, when the ship bearing his new home slipped into San Francisco Bay at the end of its long voyage 'round the Horn, it was a momentous if unheralded occasion: the Victorian house was making its West Coast debut.

Vallejo's ready-made, one of three identical cottages on board, was among the first dwellings in California to display the picturesque style and fanciful ornament that would dominate architecture on the Pacific for the next half century. Modest by comparison with some of the flamboyant homes that were to follow, it was, nonetheless, a harbinger of things to come. Gothic cottages were just the beginning. They soon gave way to larger and more ornate dwellings in the Italianate and French Second Empire styles. These in turn yielded to Stick and Eastlake houses. And by century's end all of the above had been subsumed in a new, eclectic broth known as the Queen Anne.

Once a beachhead had been established in the Bay Area, Victorian style spread up and down the coast with amazing speed. Fast on the heels of the forty-niners came loggers, carpenters, builders, architects. Hastily erected sawmills were soon busy milling the lumber needed for proper houses. Basic, clapboard boxes were the rule, of course, but whenever a touch of flair, elegance, or pure ostentation was desired, artisans turned to one of the evocative architectural modes we now recognize as indisputably Victorian. In a surprisingly short time, towers, turrets, and wooden fancywork of all sorts had become a distinctive part of the built environment in communities from Eureka to San Diego.

Why did California embrace Victoriana so enthusiastically? Part of the reason was that in architecture—as in other respects—the new state was still a frontier. Aside from the rosary of missions that dotted its southern and central coasts, it had little in the way of historic buildings to counter the picturesque revival that was sweeping the rest of America. The East Coast, which had a well-established architectural tradition—a wealth of Colonial, Federal, and Greek Revival houses—was better able to resist the Victorian tide. Pre-adolescent California, by contrast, was more than ripe for the latest architectural trends.

Add the feverish bonanza mentality that the gold seekers brought to this once sleepy Mexican outpost, and the stage was set for an extraordinary spate of building. Indeed, the unselfconscious élan of *Victoriana Pacifica* often startled visitors from the Atlantic side of the continent. Fired by gold and timber riches, and utterly unrestrained by tradition, architects like the Newsom brothers of San Francisco designed baroque confections the like of which had never been seen on the East Coast, much less in England.

As always, the most elaborate homes belonged to the richest men—railroad and shipping tycoons, lumber barons, and the occasional prospector who made a strike and managed to keep it. But in accord with some architectural version of the trickle-down theory, the more

Vallejo House, "Lachryma Montis," Sonoma, c.1850

Morey Mansion, Redlands, 1890

modest homes of doctors, lawyers, and merchants also participated in the general euphoria. Even humble clapboard cottages often displayed some hint of the decoration now seen as emblematic of the era. One-story houses with towers were not uncommon.

Many theories have been advanced to explain this architectural exuberance. The social critic Thorstein Veblen saw it as a manifestation of "conspicuous consumption"—one-upping the Joneses. Others suggested that its appearance in California was an early assertion of regional destiny—an announcement to the East that a new locus of power and culture was on the rise on the shores of the Pacific. Still others maintained that these ebullient homes, churches, and commercial buildings were nothing less than architectural expressions of the giddy, turbulent times in which they were born.

Whatever the reasons may be, it is evident that Victoriana enjoyed an extraordinary efflorescence in late nineteenth-century California: old books, newspapers and photographs attest to the fact. But more immediate evidence can be found in the mute testimony of the survivors themselves—centenarian dwellings that have run (are *still* running) the temporal gauntlet. It should go without saying that most of their kind have not been so fortunate. In fact, the vast majority of Victorian-era homes have long since succumbed to the sundry threats that continually haunt old houses—fire, dry rot, and the incessant demands of progress.

Still, as the photographs in this book suggest, the Golden State has managed to preserve a fine if uneven sampling of architectural treasures from its gilded past. San Francisco, of course, has long been recognized as a bastion of Victoriana, but many smaller cities also take pride in the wealth of historical buildings they have maintained. Even Los Angeles, home of the fast lane, harbors small enclaves where nineteenth-century structures lead precarious lives in the shadows of the freeways. Indeed, despite the continuous and rapacious development that has dominated its modern history, California possesses what is arguably the finest collection of well-preserved Victorian homes to be found in any of the fifty states.

In recent years these lucky survivors have been garnering lots of attention and approval, but this wasn't always the case. For most of the twentieth century hardly anyone had a good word to say about them. Historians dismissed them; social critics derided them; modern architects despised them. They were the unfortunate relics of a flawed social order—and bad architecture to boot. For the average person they were fussy and neurotic, quaint at best.

For the past few decades, however, new generations have been inclined to take fonder and more appreciative second looks at nineteenth-century buildings. The whimsical charm and picturesque design of the Victorian period has been especially beguiling to those reared on a strict ration of modern architecture. What is more, the most recent crop of architects and historians has begun to issue belated praise for Victorian contributions to the art and science of building.

All this is well and good, but on the eve of the millennium another, more compelling reason for this new-found popularity suggests itself—the historical continuity that vintage architecture bestows upon our all-too-modern times. In an age when the only constant seems to be change itself, it is somehow encouraging to know that houses like the one General Vallejo erected in Sonoma more than a century ago are still with us today.

The Victorian House in California

Gothic Arrivals

It is perhaps significant that the house General Vallejo selected for his country seat was a virtual paradigm of the Gothic Revival style. His choice may have been a sort of architectural pledge of allegiance to the culture and country that thrust itself upon him in 1848.

Vallejo had made his fortune in California real estate and at a relatively young age settled down to what he supposed would be a life of provincial politics and viticultural experiments. But his semi-retirement was short lived. Behind the Mexican-American War of 1846 loomed the threat—and promise—of American annexation.

As a long-time admirer of the United States and a disgruntled critic of the government in Mexico City, Vallejo argued publicly for the lopsided merger as the fastest and surest means of bringing democracy to his beloved California. Not long afterwards, the treaty of Guadalupe Hidalgo brought him his wish. He later had reason to voice some regrets, but at the time everything seemed rosy. As if to seal the compact, he married off two of his daughters to a pair of Yankee emigrants, the brothers Frisbie, and ordered a prefabricated cottage from Boston.

Lachryma Montis, as he called it, still dominates the Sonoma homestead *(p. 6)* that has since become a state historical park. As for its siblings, one has disappeared, but another, the Frisbie-Walsh House, is still standing in Benicia, where, restored after years of neglect, it now serves as a bed and breakfast. A fourth cottage, similar to the others in plan—and identical in some details—can be found in Strafford, Vermont, where it was built in 1851 by Justin Smith Morrill, the U.S. Congressman who sponsored the Land Grant College Act.

Although its source has not been positively established, the design of the four houses bears the general stamp of Andrew Jackson Downing—landscape gardener, author, and America's premier architectural tastemaker in the mid-nineteenth century. As he made clear in his books and his journal, *The Horticulturist*, Downing thought the Gothic Revival an especially appropriate style for his countrymen: its simplicity reflected their egalitarian ideals, and its picturesque massing complemented the rough-hewn landscape they were settling. Apparently many people shared this view. Beginning in the late 1830s, the Gothic star was on the rise, and by the end of the 1840s it had eclipsed the Greek Revival as the preeminent architectural mode for rural residences in the Northeast and Midwest.

As a well-read devotee of horticultural science, Vallejo was probably aware of these opinions. In any case, *Lachryma Montis* perfectly fills Downing's prescription for the country home of a gentleman with democratic leanings: it is ample and stylish but not at all pretentious.

The *Vallejo House* and its twin in Benicia were not the only prefabricated houses to be built in California's early Victorian period, nor are they the only surviving specimens. *The Captain Watkins House* in Atherton and the *Callen-Rhodes House* in Woodland *(p. 11)* are two others that are still standing today. Most of the rest, however, have long since faded away.

Towle House, Bridgeport, 1878

Captain Watkins House, Atherton, 1860

MacCallum House, Mendocino, 1882

Stevinson House, Pacific Grove, 1883

Callen-Rhodes-Laugenour House, Woodland, 1873

Transplanted Yankees were another source of Gothic styling on the West Coast. In Mendocino, where many state of Mainers settled, the Gothic is a dominant stylistic note *(pp. 11, 28)*. The *Towle House (p. 10)* in the small eastern Sierra community of Bridgeport is the work of another Maine lumberman.

But despite these and some other interesting examples scattered around the state, it must be said that the Gothic Revival was never as popular in California as in the East. Part of the reason may be that the Gothic tide had already peaked by the time settlement of the West Coast began in earnest. Another limiting factor was the style's strong identification with rural architecture. As a result it was seldom employed in San Francisco, which, especially in the early years, set the architectural tone for the rest of the state. As for the countryside, the Gothic was eclipsed by another early Victorian style—the Italianate. In the gold-mining country, the urgency of early building demanded a simpler, more immediate style.

For expedient housing, nothing matched the vernacular clapboard shacks favored by semi-transient miners and the merchants, working girls, and flimflam artists who dogged their tracks.

Although the Gothic fever was waning by the time California became part of the American enterprise, the style continued to exert a powerful and persistent influence on building in the state for the rest of the nineteenth century. Pure examples may be rare, but Gothic elements can be found in structures as variously formed and widely separated as the *Lucky Baldwin House* in Arcadia *(p. 72)* and the *William Carson Mansion* in Eureka *(pp. 2, 29)*. Nor should we forget the churches, especially the Episcopalian ones: in nineteenth-century California, the Gothic Revival was the overwhelming mode of choice for ecclesiastic architecture. Indeed, the purest expressions of board-and-batten architecture remaining in the state today can be found in some of the churches that have survived in the Mother Lode country *(p. 68)*.

Italian Villas

In California's early Victorian period it was another picturesque mode—the Italianate—that dominated country houses. One reason was the climate. The state's hot, sun-drenched valleys were more akin to Italy's *Campagna* than to the craggy New York wilderness that A. J. Downing knew best. Broad-eaved, flat-roofed Italianate dwellings were admirably suited both to the weather and to the lifestyles of successful ranchers and growers. Never mind that most such houses were American copies of English adaptations of vernacular Italian originals. Like the Gothic, they had Downing's stamp of approval. Although he preferred the latter for cottages, he thought the Italianate particularly appropriate for the country homes of sophisticated men of the world. He also noted its special suitability for southern climes.

An early exemplar of the style still standing today is the *General John Bidwell Mansion,* completed in Chico in 1867 *(p. 46)*. In 1841 Bidwell had led the first party of overland settlers to the Sacramento Valley. He prospered nicely as a farmer for several years, but when news of the gold strikes reached him in 1848, he hastened to the Sierras, where he acquired the wealth that enabled him to build his expansive country seat. Designed by a well-known eastern architect, Henry Cleaveland, the mansion has most of the earmarks of the Italianate—low-pitched roofs, rounded or segmental arched windows, hood-molds, eaves-brackets, and a central tower, to name a few of the most prominent.

The architectural historian Harold Kirker has called the Bidwell House "the representative example of the Italian Villa on the Pacific frontier." His assessment may be correct, but from the 1870s on, there was no shortage of well-appointed Italianate residences in rural and small-town California. Even today quite a number of survivors can be found throughout the state. The *Kelly-Griggs House* in Red Bluff, the *Perry House* in Los Angeles, a number of interesting examples in Napa and National City, and an especially rich cluster of villas and near-villas in Woodland *(p. 49)* testify to the popularity of the style in rural and suburban California.

As for the city, San Francisco has a collection of Italianate dwellings unmatched in number, quality, and diversity anywhere in America. True, the largest and most lavish exponents of the style—the great mansions of the Victorian rich and famous on and around Nob Hill—have entirely disappeared. Many were razed in the great earthquake and fire of 1906, and those that survived that calamity later succumbed to an even greater one—progress. Nonetheless, San Francisco still retains block upon block of fine if less imposing Italianate homes. In the 1870s and early 1880s, the style came close to shutting out all competition as the preferred mode for row and townhouses. Of the thousands that were built, hundreds survived the 1906 blaze west of the fire line. Thanks to a combination of benign neglect and positive restoration efforts, many are still standing today.

The Evolution of the Row House

As in eastern cities, the earliest townhouses in San Francisco were basic, end-gabled, frame boxes, more or less devoid of stylistic references. Typically they rose two stories above a raised basement and had a narrow front divided into three parts: a third each for an off-center doorway and two windows. The simplicity of these structures invited stylistic embellishment. In their decorative details row and townhouses followed the same stylistic course as their suburban and country cousins. From minimal beginnings, they acquired Italianate, Second Empire, Stick, Eastlake, Queen Anne, and Classical Revival trappings.

However, unlike freestanding houses whose forms often changed with the ornament, row houses retained their narrow plan and tripartite facade arrangement throughout the century. The examples shown on the next several pages illustrate some of the stages on the road from Italianate to Free Classic. To Italicize a basic, flat-front row or townhouse, a builder or renovator had only to add a few stylistic touches—cornice brackets, round-headed windows, decorative door and window surrounds, and a small hood over the entry.

The result was an Italianate row house similar to the one pictured on page 14. Flat fronts were popular until the mid 1870s when—either through remodeling or in new construction—they began to change into bay fronts. The transformation typically took place as follows. On one side of the facade, the paired windows on the first and second floors would push out to form a two-story bay window. On the other side, the hood over the doorway developed into a freestanding portico, usually surmounted by a small balcony. The Italianate details remained

Flat-Front Townhouse, San Francisco, c.1883

Bay-Front Townhouse, San Francisco, 1876

Eastlake Townhouse, San Francisco, 1888

Vollmer House, San Francisco, 1885

essentially the same over time, but grew in size and complexity. Cornice brackets multiplied, classical porch columns appeared, decorative quoins simulating masonry replaced the simple corner boards of earlier models.

As the Stick and Eastlake styles came into vogue in the 1880s, facades became even busier and more ornate. Vertical stick-work tied the window surrounds to the eaves brackets, and cornice panels replicated themselves and took root wherever they could find an unrelieved wall surface. Tentatively at first, then profusely, spindle courses and split-spindle appliqué appeared. Meanwhile, the rounded bays of the 1870s were squared off and enlarged. (Eventually they projected so far out over the sidewalk that the city had to pass ordinances limiting their extension.) At the top of the structure a false front might take on a mansardic or gabled disguise, but until late in the century the actual roof was apt to be flat or low pitched.

By the mid 1890s, new townhouses were borrowing some decorative tricks from the suburban Queen Anne—shingle cladding, spindlework, sunbursts, and leaded windows. Toward the end of the century some sprouted turrets and acquired thick columns, Palladian windows, and other trappings associated with the "Free Classic" and Shingle styles.

Mansard Palaces

Beginning in the 1870s the French Second Empire became *de rigueur* as a style for the mansions of the Victorian *nouveau riche*. These sophisticated transplants from Baron Hausmann's Paris had ornamental features—sills, lintels, brackets, and so on—that were quite similar to those found in Italianate structures. The true hallmark of the Second Empire was a distinctive, two-sloped mansard roof.

Since a mansard added nearly as much space to a structure as an additional story, it had been adopted in Paris as a way of side-stepping zoning laws that limited buildings to six floors. But in America it soon became a mark of distinction. A mansard roof atop a house signaled that its owner was—or wanted to be—wealthy, sophisticated and well traveled. In the East old money might scoff at these parvenu pretensions, but in California there was no old money to speak of. To bonanza kings and railroad barons the French Second Empire seemed the perfect style in which to dress a mansion.

But of the extraordinary mansard palaces built in San Francisco and elsewhere in Victorian California, precious little remains today. Even before 1900, residences in "The General Grant Style" had fallen from favor. Those that survived into the new century were generally regarded as egregious white elephants, unfortunate reminders of the robber-baron era. In general they were demolished without remorse or apology. In San Francisco most of them had already perished in the catastrophe of 1906. Aside from some mansardic townhouses in that city—and the *Old Governor's Mansion* in Sacramento *(p. 20)*—the Second Empire style in California is today represented mainly by a smaller, less haughty relative: the French cottage. This subgenre retained the mansard but added porches and other informal touches. The *Reed-Lyford House* in Tiburon *(p. 35)*, the *McPheters House* in Santa Cruz *(p. 20)* and the *Shaw House* in Los Angeles are among the scattered examples that have survived.

Queen Anne Row House, San Francisco, c.1895

Free Classic Townhouse, San Francisco, c.1898

17

Stick and Eastlake

The Stick style, which gained popularity in the late 1870s, represented a turn back to the Gothic Revival. The architects of that period, in fact, often referred to it as "Modern Gothic." In the East Stick style houses generally had tall, angular profiles with steep-pitched roofs and sharply-pointed gables. Elaborate trusses and square towers were also common. But the defining characteristic of the style was a distinctive type of ornament that included thin vertical battens and stylized cross braces. Vincent Scully, Jr., who coined the term, saw this patterning as an extension of the board-and-batten tradition of the Gothic Revival. He took its reappearance as a sign of renewed interest in the ideals of structural honesty that had been partially submerged during Victoriana's flirtation with Italianate and Second Empire forms. The decorative posts, beams, and braces that adorned the outer skin of the structure pointed to and reflected the underlying frame that supported it.

Vintage photographs show that Stick style abodes were common in San Francisco and other California cities in the 1880s and 1890s, but relatively few examples have survived in pure form. The *Sherman-Gilbert House (p. 55)*, a highly stylized residence in San Diego, is one example. The extraordinary *Pitkin House* in Arroyo Grande *(p. 21)* also qualifies by dint of its tall proportions and square tower. Some other fairly pure examples can be found around the state, but most Stick style houses seem to have been remodeled to reflect later ornamental schemes.

In fact it seems that California largely skipped over the Stick style in pursuit of one of its offshoots: Eastlake. More a decorative mode than a style per se, Eastlake derived both from the Stick patterning of the board-and-batten tradition and from the furniture motifs of an influential English designer, Charles Locke Eastlake. His *Hints on Household Taste* (1872), included illustrations of interiors decorated with incised wooden panels, linear stripping, and rows of knob-like projections. These devices were supposed to complement his furniture designs, but in America—particularly in San Francisco—some of them began to appear on the *exteriors* of houses as well.

The resulting style came to be known as "Eastlake," much to the chagrin of its originator. Sir Charles was quick to repudiate the American fashion that had appropriated his name. "Extravagant and bizarre" was his assessment of the upstart architecture. But the term stuck, and in California, more than in any other part of the United States, the distinctive ornament became a mainstay of late-Victorian architecture.

In the Americanized version, decorative elements were mass produced on steam-powered milling machines. Lathe-turned spindlework, a hallmark of the Eastlake style, replaced the flat-cut gingerbread of earlier decades. Full spindles were used to create decorative spindle courses and elaborate balusters; split spindles were applied to panels and wall surfaces to create fans, sunbursts, and other motifs.

By the 1880s architects and builders were combining Eastlake details with Italianate and Second Empire elements to produce a new synthesis that came to be known as the "San Franciso Style." Inventive designers like the Newsom brothers exploited these elements to create some remarkably eclectic buildings. But the single most important element of the "San Francisco Style" was structural, not decorative. The bay window may have been invented elsewhere, but it achieved its greatest success in San Francisco. Harold Kirker reports that 95 percent of the buildings built in the city between 1867 and 1885 had a bay window of one sort or another. In a seaside environment that was often fog-bound and light-starved, these framed "prows of glass" came to be regarded as necessities.

Another California specialty—redwood—deserves brief mention here. As the building material of choice, it had a great influence on architecture in the Golden State. Dense, strong, eminently workable, and in those days still plentiful, it lent itself readily to the sort of ornament that was later damned as Victorian excess. The culmination of this decorative largess is illustrated in California's most famous redwood palace, the William Carson Mansion *(pp. 2, 29)*.

Besides its workability, redwood has another outstanding attribute—its famed resistance to rot, decay, and insects. Its frequent use as a construction material throughout California helps explain the longevity as well as the extravagance of many of the state's vintage homes.

Old Governor's Mansion, Sacramento, 1874

McPheters House, Santa Cruz, 1882

Pitkin House, Arroyo Grande, 1885

Queen Anne Villas

The Victorian Queen Anne Revival initially drew inspiration from some rather plain, hip-roofed, Dutch dwellings that had come to England with William III at the end of the seventeenth century. The English architect Richard Norman Shaw is credited with creating the revival style, and the American architect Henry Hobson Richardson is usually cited as the first to employ it on this side of the Atlantic. But the wood-frame Queen Anne house that dominated domestic architecture in America from the mid 1880s to the end of the century bore only token resemblance to its high-art progenitors. This often led to confusion. "Queen Anne," wrote a nineteenth-century architectural commentator, "is a comprehensive name which has been made to cover a multitude of incongruities, including, indeed, the bulk of recent work which otherwise defies description."

The popularized American version was an ample, horizontal, hipped-roof affair with irregular massing and rambling, free-flowing floor plans. Corner towers or turrets were common. So were fluted chimney stacks, leaded glass windows, and an abundance of surface detail—stick patterning, spindlework, patterned shingles. By the end of the century, residences that fit this description could be found in every corner of the United States, California not excepted.

In San Francisco, row and townhouses began dressing themselves in Queen Anne finery in the 1890s. But as early as the mid eighties the style had found employment in the modish demi-mansions of the city's Western Addition. Since much of the area lay west of the 1906 fire line, some of them—notably the *Haas-Lilienthal Mansion (p. 38)*—are still standing today.

Other northern towns—Alameda, Eureka, San Jose, Santa Rosa—soon followed San Francisco's stylistic lead.

But it was in Southern California, which was just coming into its own, that the Queen Anne found an especially warm reception. As late as 1880 Los Angeles was hardly more than an oversized cow town, a place known chiefly for beef and hides and as a haven for northern fugitives. But in the decade that followed, the area bloomed, thanks to the arrival of railroads, land speculators, and citrus growers. In 1887 a real-estate boom engineered by railroad and land interests brought masses of home buyers to Los Angeles for the first time. The bubble soon burst, but new ones were manufactured every few years for the rest of the century and into the next.

During the ensuing orgy of development the Queen Anne villa reigned supreme. Its broad dimensions and freedom of plan were eminently suited to the nearer suburbs of growing towns like Los Angeles and San Diego. Moreover, the warm climate allowed it to indulge another of its predilections—extended, wraparound porches—that would have been impractical and uncomfortable in fog-prone San Francisco.

One of the earliest residences in the Los Angeles area to flirt with Queen Anne styling was the *Lucky Baldwin House* of 1876 *(p. 72)*. Designed by A. A. Bennett, it displays a wealth of flat-cut gingerbread that is essentially Gothic in tone. But its freedom of plan, its broad verandahs and its pavilion-capped tower capture the essence of the Queen Anne villa to be. Later and more typical examples can be seen in several surviving residences in Angelino Heights. *(pp. 56, 57)*

The boom in the south drew northern builders, developers, and architects like bears to honey. This infusion of established talent had the effect of unifying the state's architecture, north and south. Prominent among the northern émigré artisans were the Newsom brothers,

Samuel and Joseph. They had already left their mark on San Francisco and Eureka when, in 1888, they opened a Los Angeles office that flourished for a decade or more. By all accounts their most fabulous residential commission in Southern California was the *Bradbury House,* sadly destroyed decades ago. But some of their other projects—the *Pinney House* in Sierra Madre *(p. 61),* the *Lewis House* in MacArthur Park and the *Sessions House (p. 65)* in Angelino Heights—are still there to be seen.

The latter two are remarkably early demonstrations of one of the transformations that overtook the Queen Anne house toward the end of the century. Built in the late 1880s, both show the influence of the Shingle style that had recently come into fashion in some of the more exclusive seaside communities in New York and New England. Custom designed and expensive to construct, Shingle style residences were correctly regarded as the province of the old-moneyed Northeast, and they never achieved mass acceptance in the rest of America. But elements of the style trickled down in the work of mainstream practitioners like the Newsoms who prided themselves on keeping up with new developments in the field. The fad of shingle-clad exterior walls that began in the late 1880s is traceable to the Shingle style, as are the broadened eaves and bow windows that appear in many late-blooming Queen Annes.

Some of these details can also be seen in the work of William Henry Weeks, a Northern California architect who melded elements of the Queen Anne and Shingle styles in some of his domestic projects. The *Julius Lee House* in Watsonville *(p. 63)* and the *Sargent House* in Salinas *(p. 65)* are two examples. Both are remarkably similar to some of the early houses Frank Lloyd Wright designed in Oak Park, Illinois at about the same time.

Another Weeks design, Watsonville's *Tuttle Mansion, (p. 62)* illustrates the second major transformation that overtook the Queen Anne style at the end of the century. This phase of its development cast the towered villa into a more solid and conservative mold than in the past. Once-slender towers became stout turrets; spindly Eastlake porch posts became Greco-Roman columns; shingle cladding and sunburst ornament gave way to acanthus and other classical motifs. These changes reflected the swing toward neoclassicism that occurred around the turn of the century. Hence the term "Free Classic" that is often applied to late Queen Anne houses.

J. M. Carson House, Eureka, 1887

Ring House, "The Gingerbread Mansion," Ferndale, 1899

Romantic Eclecticism

The classification of the Victorian styles into neat categories—Gothic, Italianate, and so on—belies the true architectural diversity of the period. In practice, motifs were often mixed to produce hybrid styles that defy precise classification. There were also some genuine anomalies. Beginning in the 1850s, for example, a minor fad for octagon houses developed thanks to an enthusiastic pamphleteer, publisher and eccentric named Orson Squire Fowler. In his *Home for All* (1848) he championed round or octagonal shapes as the most fitting for physical and spiritual living. Since only a few thousand octagons were built throughout the country during the nineteenth century, it is remarkable that two of them are still standing in San Francisco.

As the century progressed, a host of other stylistic influences—Chateauesque, Romanesque, even Egyptian—added their voices to the Victorian choir. In California, gateway to the Orient, the exotic East sometimes met the Victorian West, as witness the extraordinary *Vedanta Society Headquarters* in San Francisco.

Fortunately or unfortunately—depending on one's point of view—most of the truly exotic experiments of the period have long since perished. Like the mansardic palaces of the 1870s they sorely tried the patience of the modernists who came to power in the early decades of the twentieth century. Generally only the more tasteful examples have managed to survive. Alfred Schroepfer's *Beringer House* in St. Helena *(p. 32)*, a rather successful attempt to bring the aesthetics of the Rhine River to California's Wine Country, is one. Another is Carroll H. Brown's *Stimson House* in Los Angeles—a rare and wonderful example of Richardsonian Romanesque styling sculpted in Arizona sandstone *(p. 73)*.

The Victorian predilection for architectural drama and whimsy was a reflection of the profound romanticism of the era. In that period, more than any other, houses straddled the border between architecture and theater. Buildings often have a symbolic function, but Victorian residences carried this a step further. No longer merely dwelling places that suggested their owners' stature and prestige, they were often conceived as virtual stage sets in which luminous ideals and happy fantasies could be hatched and nurtured.

The architecture of the period was also an interregnum in the neoclassical movement that dominated the eighteenth and early nineteenth centuries. The Gothic Revival had swept away the Greek Revival and replaced its residue of orderly classicism with picturesque forms derived from accounts, largely fictional, of medieval life. But throughout the last half of the nineteenth century neoclassicism continually tried to reassert itself. It achieved its greatest success in the more-or-less classical decoration that often attached itself to formal residences of Italianate and Second Empire persuasion. But until the end of the century it had not pierced the Gothic citadel itself. When, in the late 1890s, classical elements infiltrated the Queen Anne style, it was a signal that the era of Gothic romanticism had run its course.

Victorian California: A Guide

The following is a brief guide to California communities where Victoriana still flourishes. It is certainly not exhaustive, but it may serve to point interested parties in the right direction.

In larger cities, serious researchers may want to consult books that offer more detailed information than can be included here. The bibliography on page 78 may be of help. These days even small towns commonly issue maps, brochures, and walking tours that highlight their architecture. Check with local visitor information services and libraries.

Some notes on what follows:
• Houses and other buildings illustrated in this book are marked with bullets and page references.
• When possible we've included phone numbers for those structures that offer tours or are otherwise open to the public. In making plans to visit, please remember that hours, fees, telephone numbers, and even area codes are apt to change.
• Except as noted, the listed houses are private residences. It should go without saying that visitors should respect the occupants' privacy.

The North Coast

The 350-mile coastline that extends from the Oregon border to the San Francisco Bay is—or used to be—redwood country. In the north, Humboldt Bay initially presented itself as a handy jumping-off place for prospectors seeking riches in the Trinity gold fields. But the good anchorage and the magnificent stands of trees in the area soon made it a logging center from which shiploads of timber were sent down the coast to supply San Francisco's continuous building booms. Not surprisingly, Eureka and Arcata, the two towns on the bay, soon began to acquire their own share of Victoriana, much of which is still standing today. Ditto for Ferndale, a dairy center which has managed to maintain much of its nineteenth-century flavor. Further south, the town of Mendocino, which also enjoyed a stint as a lumber center, retains some interesting vernacular adaptations of the Gothic Revival style.

Arcata

Toward the end of the last century Arcata lost out to Eureka in its bid for supremacy on Humboldt Bay. As a result, the town has been able to retain some Victorian homes and commercial buildings—centered around the town square off 7th Street—that might otherwise have been lost to progress.

Jackson-Matthews House, 1888. 980 14th. Builder: Theodore Dean. One of two reversed-plan, corner-towered Queen Anne villas that bracket 14th Street like a set of bookends.

• **Stone House**, 1888. 902 14th. The other half of the pair. This one has become a bed and breakfast: *The Lady Anne.* 707-822-2797. **p. 28.**

• **Bair-Stokes House**, 1888. 916 13th. Builder: Shepherd Hall. A corner-towered Queen Anne with an elaborate horseshoe-arched porch. Originally the home of a local doctor, it was later the residence of lumberman Thomas Bair, a self-made millionaire. **p. 60.**

Blair House, Mendocino, 1888

Stone House, "The Lady Anne," Arcata, 1888

William Carson Mansion, Eureka, 1886

Eureka

In the mid 1880s lumberman William McKendrie Carson brought the Newsom brothers to town and commissioned them to design a residence. The result of this combination of money and talent was a mansion that has become the most celebrated Victorian in the state, if not the country. The Newsoms are credited with several other Eureka houses from the same period, but what may be the most surprising example of their talent—the *Carter House*—is of more recent vintage. Given all this, it is not surprising that some of the best surviving exponents of the "San Francisco Style" are to be found in Eureka. The town has more well-preserved Victoriana than can be mentioned here. Some highlights:

• **William Carson Mansion**, 1886. 2nd and M. Architects: Samuel and Joseph Cather Newsom. A High Victorian tour de force built by and for Eureka's premiere lumber baron. Basically Queen Anne, it synthesized most of the foregoing Victorian styles in a virtuoso display of picturesque massing and baroque ornament. The scale of this landmark allowed the architects a full canvas on which to realize their penchants for ornamental complexity and bold statement of form. It was probably also meant as a demonstration of the capabilities of redwood as a construction and ornamental material. Carson, it is said, wanted to keep his workers busy during a lull in the timber business. It is now a private club. ***pp. 2, 29.***

• **J. Milton Carson House**, 1897. 202 M. Architects: S. & J. Newsom. An exceptional corner-towered Queen Anne with elaborate Eastlake decoration. Built for the son of William Carson, it is now an office building. ***p. 24.***

Young House, c.1893. 1006 2nd. Builder: O. F. Mowry. A gabled-ell, Queen Anne cottage that was truncated when it was relocated from Hillsdale Street a few years back.

• **Carter House Inn**, c.1980. 1033 3rd. Architects: S. & J. Newsom. Modern builder Mark Carter used original Newsom plans to execute this faithful, redwood facsimile of San Francisco's *Murphy House* (1885). The original had perished in the great earthquake and fire of 1906. 707-445-1390. ***p. 53***

Boyd House, 1885. 409 4th. Architects: S. & J. Newsom. Eastlake in style but altered since original construction. A drawing of this house is featured in the Newsoms' first pattern book, *Picturesque California Homes.*

Eastlake Cottage, c.1885. 1305 6th. A raised-basement house with a corner turret and elaborately turned window brackets.

• **W. S. Clark House**, 1888. 1406 C. Builder: F. B. Butterfield. Eastlake abundance overlaying a double-bayed, raised-basement cottage. In recent years it has become *An Elegant Victorian Mansion,* a bed and breakfast establishment. 707-442-5594. ***p. 50.***

Free Classic House, c.1898. 1604 G. A late Queen Anne residence with Classical Revival embellishments.

Hillsdale Street

In its two short blocks this street displays a virtual catalog of suburban, gabled-ell cottages, all similar in plan but in a full range of styles. It's off E Street between 12th and 13th.

• **A. W. Torrey House**, 1893. 216 Hillsdale. Builder: F. Mowry. A gabled Queen Anne with an elaborate spindle course framing the porch. ***p. 56.***

• **G. W. Morse House**, 1889. 233 Hillsdale. Here the style is Eastlake. ***p. 52.***

Layton House, 1892. 258 Hillsdale. Builder: A. Redmond. Italianate with Stick and Eastlake embellishments.

Ferndale

South of Eureka, just off Highway 101, is a Victorian village as authentic and well maintained as any to be found in the United States. Since its beginnings the town has flourished as a dairy center. Its isolated location has allowed it to retain its original character despite the winds of change. To help keep itself on the straight and narrow in the future, Ferndale applied for and was granted historical status some years back. Among the notable structures in town are dozens of interesting homes including several that have become bed and breakfasts. It also has two fine churches, many commercial buildings, and the most charming main street this side of Disneyland—but this one is real.

• **Ring House**, 1899. 400 Berding. A spindlework confection designed and built by a local doctor, Hogan J. Ring. It is now *The Gingerbread Mansion Bed & Breakfast.* 707-786-4000. *p. 25.*

Old Berding House, 1875. 455 Ocean. Victorian Gothic with Stick style accretions.

• **Eastlake storefront**, *The Gazebo*, 1898. 475 Main. A sumptuous and elaborate storefront with Stick and Eastlake details, some of them gilded. It was originally Red Star Clothing. *p. 52.*

Church of the Assumption, 1896. 546 Berding. An exceptionally fine Victorian Gothic church.

Shaw House, c.1866. 703 Main. The Gothic Revival residence of Seth Shaw is reputedly the oldest building in "Cream City." It is now the *Shaw House Bed & Breakfast.* 707-786-9958.

• **L. M. Smith House**, 1894. 923 Main. A well-preserved residence with elaborate Eastlake details. Despite his name, Mr. Smith was actually a cooper who worked for one of Ferndale's several creameries. *p. 51.*

Mendocino

Mendocino began as a lumber town in 1852, but its commercially viable timber was depleted within a few decades. For most of the twentieth century it languished, but in the 1960s it was rediscovered and has since become a most cultivated backwater, home to numerous artists and musicians.

The influence of the many New Englanders who originally settled the area is evident in the Gothic-tinged vernacular structures that have survived. The entire town was granted historical status some years back.

• **MacCallum House**, 1882. 740 Albion. A late-blooming Gothic Revival cottage, originally the home of Alexander and Daisy MacCallum. It is now the *MacCallum House Restaurant and Inn.* 707-937-0289. *p. 11.*

• **Blair House**, 1888. 45110 Little Lake. Builder: John D. Johnson. The spirit of the Gothic Revival is apparent in the steep gables and board-and-batten siding displayed in this expanded cottage. It was originally the residence of Elisha Blair, a mill worker and former state of Mainer. When building tapered off in Mendocino, carpenter Johnson turned to a more depression-proof trade—undertaking. The former Blair residence is now a bed and breakfast. 707-937-1800. *p. 28.*

Presbyterian Church, 1868. Main St. near Howard. A picturesque, board-and-batten Gothic Revival church that has served as a location for more than a few movies. Like most of the other buildings in town it was constructed of locally milled redwood. Construction cost? A mere $7,000.

Little River

Little River Inn, 1853. 7751 N. Hwy. 1. A multi-gabled Gothic Revival inn. 707-937-5942.

Beringer "Rhine" House, St. Helena, 1883

Sonoma, Napa, and Marin

The wine districts of Sonoma and Napa Counties have a range of architecture that runs the gamut of Victorian styles from Rural Gothic (General Vallejo's *Lachryma Montis*) to Richardsonian Romanesque (*The Christian Brothers Winery*). The area is especially well endowed with Italianate villas, and in Santa Rosa and Petaluma there are some interesting Eastlake and Queen Anne houses. The most Victorian-rich site in Wine Country is the town of Napa, which has a host of very interesting homes in a variety of styles and flavors, mostly—alas—tree shrouded.

Further south, in Marin County, most of the surviving Victoriana is hidden and inaccessible. But San Rafael has some interesting homes, including one by the Newsoms, and the picturesque *Reed-Lyford House* in Tiburon is not to be missed.

Healdsburg

Paxton House, 1881. 1001 Westside Rd. An imposing, mansard-roofed pile. Originally the summer place of a wealthy San Franciscan, it is now the *Madrona Manor Hotel & Restaurant:* 707-433-4231.

Powell-Seawall House, 1869. 211 North. A flat-front Italianate townhouse. Now *The Camelia Inn:* 707-433-8182.

Calistoga

A. C. Palmer House, 1871. 1300 Cedar. The French Second Empire home of Calistoga's first circuit judge. It may have been derived from one of the pattern books published by A. J. Bicknell. It is now *Elms,* a bed and breakfast:* 707-942-9476.

St. Helena

• **Beringer *Rhine* House**, 1883. 2000 Main. Architect: Alfred Schroepfer. A "Rhinish" castle based on the Beringer family home in Mainz, Germany. It is usually open for wine tasting and tours. 707-963-4812. ***p. 32.***

Christian Brothers Winery, 1889. Hwy. 29 North. Architects: Percy and Hamilton. Richardsonian Romanesque.

Santa Rosa

McDonald Mansion, *Mableton,* 1876. 1015 McDonald. An interesting structure, indisputably Victorian, but hard to pin down as to style. It was once the home of Mark Lindsay McDonald, an early Santa Rosa developer.

Wright House, c. 1888. 815 McDonald. Queen Anne with Eastlake details.

Roberts House, 1877. 4257 Petaluma Hill Rd. The multi-gabled High Victorian Gothic residence of William Roberts, an early settler. It is now *The Gables,* a bed and breakfast. 707-585-7777.

Sonoma

• **General Mariano Vallejo House**, *Lachryma Montis,* c.1850. West Spain at 3rd. One of three identical, prefabricated Gothic revival cottages shipped 'round the Horn from Boston during the gold rush era. Its surviving twin is the *Captain Walsh House* in Benicia. Decorated and furnished authentically, the Vallejo House is now a California State Historic Landmark open to the public. 707-938-1578. ***p. 6.***

Shwarz-Birnheim House, "La Belle Epoque," Napa, 1893

William Andrews House, Napa, 1892

Double Bay house, Napa, c.1885

Reed-Lyford House, Tiburon, 1874

Napa

• **William Andrews House**, 1892. 741 Seminary. Architect: Luther Turton. An Eastlake-bedizened Queen Anne designed and built for a miller and grocer who emigrated from England. *p. 34.*

• **Shwarz-Birnheim House**, 1893. 1386 Calistoga. A raised-basement cottage with some of the same Eastlake ornament seen in the Andrews House. Now *La Belle Epoque,* a bed and breakfast. 707-257-2161. *p. 34.*

Italianate House, c.1875. 313 Franklin. Notwithstanding its irregular facade, this house has a decidedly formal presence.

• **Double Bay House**, c.1885. 330 Randolph. A raised cottage with Eastlake and Italianate details. *p. 34.*

Queen Anne House, c.1888. 492 Randolph. A large, corner-towered Queen Anne residence.

Petaluma

Eastlake Style House, c.1890. 219 Kentucky. Basically Queen Anne with Eastlake details.

Bodega

Bodega Schoolhouse, c.1873. 17110 Bodega Lane. The Italianate schoolhouse used in Alfred Hitchcock's film, *The Birds.*

San Rafael

Falkirk Cultural Center, 1888. 1408 Mission. Architect: Clinton Day. An ample Queen Anne residence. Tours by appointment. 415-485-3328.

• **Shingled Cottage**, c.1887. 230 Forbes. Architects: S. & J. Newsom. Queen Anne leaning toward the Shingle style. Note the "moon-gate" porch reminiscent of the *Sessions House* in Los Angeles. *p. 65.*

Tiburon

• **Reed-Lyford House**, 1874. 376 Greenwood Beach Rd. French Second Empire home of the physician and dairy farmer Benjamin Lyford and his wife, Hilarita Reed. Moved from Strawberry Point and restored by architect John Lord King in 1957, it is now the headquarters of the Marin Chapter of the Audubon Society. *p. 35.*

The Bay Area

As the fount of American culture on the West Coast, the San Francisco Bay Area is especially well endowed with Victoriana of all stripes and persuasions. Many books have been devoted to the city itself, but some of her neighbors in the East Bay—particularly Alameda—contain nineteenth-century enclaves that have received less attention. To the south, the peninsula also has a number of noteworthy houses.

San Francisco

It goes without saying that San Francisco is the chief reliquary of Victoriana in the country. If most of the city's nineteenth-century architecture was destroyed in the catastrophe of 1906, enough remains today to make it a mecca for devotees of nineteenth-century architecture.

During the first half of the twentieth century many of the city's Victorians languished in a state of benign neglect, but in the late 1960s the colorist movement and a renewed interest in historical architecture sparked serious renovation and restoration efforts. Today, beautifully restored homes can be found in the Western Addition, Pacific Heights, Haight-Ashbury, and the Mission District. Besides block upon block of row and townhouses along Castro, Steiner and many other streets, there are a number of freestanding mansions that testify to the opulence of former times. Serious Victorian hunters will want to consult one of the several comprehensive guides to the city's architecture. A few highlights appear below.

Mission District

Row Houses, c.1880. 120-126 Guerrero. A well preserved group of bay-front Italianate row houses.

• **Flat-Front Row House**, c.1883. 135 Castro. Though built in the 1880s, this Italianate row house is more typical of the 1870s. *p. 14.*

Row Houses, c.1890. 725-733 Castro. Builder: Fernando Nelson. A group of Stick-Eastlake row houses.

Western Addition

• **Westerfeld House**, 1889. 1198 Fulton. Architect: Henry Geilfuss. An imposing towered villa in the San Francisco eclectic style. Designed vertically to fit on a narrow urban lot, it was originally the home of confectioner William Westerfeld. *p. 38.*

• **Queen Anne Row House**, c.1890. 700 block Steiner. Builder Matthew Kavanaugh. One of a half dozen freestanding houses arranged as a terrace—a row house group unified by an overall design scheme. *p. 17.*

• **Queen Anne Townhouse**, c.1898. 850 Steiner. The townhouse in its "Free Classic" phase. *p. 17.*

• **Eastlake Townhouse**, 1888. 908 Steiner. Architects: Schmidt & Shea. A townhouse with rectangular bay windows and a combination of Italianate, Stick, and Eastlake details typical of the 1880s. It was originally the home of Nels Everson, a lumber dealer. *p. 15.*

• **Vollmer House**, 1885. 1737 Webster. Architects: S. & J. Newsom. A post-Eastlake masterpiece, this townhouse was relocated and restored by the Foundation for San Francisco's Architectural Heritage. It is, reputedly, the only building designed by the Newsoms that is still standing in San Francisco. *p. 15.*

Pacific Heights

• **Haas-Lilienthal House**, 1886. 2007 Franklin. Architect: Peter Schmidt. A splendid Queen Anne mansion located less than two hundred yards from the line where the fire of 1906 was brought to a halt. Now headquarters for the Foundation for San Francisco's Architectural Heritage, it is open for public tours. 415-441-3004. *p. 38.*

Double-Bay House, c.1875. 1782 Pacific. A bracketed, double-bay Italianate house with central portico and balcony. It was originally the San Francisco residence of a Pacific Northwest lumber baron.

• **Sloss House**, 1876. 2026 California. A splendid example of the bay-front Italianate townhouse, complete with brackets, portico, and quoined corners. *p. 14.*

Sussman-Coleman House, 1876. 1834 California. Originally Italianate, but revamped in 1895 to reflect the Classical Revival.

Vedanta Society Headquarters, 1905. Webster at Filbert. Architect: J. A. Leonard with an assist from Swami Trigunatitananda. An eccentric melding of East and West—late Queen Anne with Mogul touches.

McElroy House, *The Octagon*, c.1852. 2645 Gough. One of San Francisco's two octagon houses. Relocated and restored by the National Society of Colonial Dames, it is open for public tours. 415-441-7512.

Italianate Row Houses, c.1875. 2637-2673 Clay. A terrace of mixed flat and bay fronts.

Townhouse, c.1910. 2413 Franklin. A narrow three-story house with French accents ranging from Second Empire to *Art Nouveau.*

Westerfeld House, San Francisco, 1889

Haas-Lilienthal House, San Francisco, 1886

Brehaut House, Alameda, 1893

The East Bay

Rampant development and redevelopment in the sprawling East Bay has tended to flatten much of the area's early architecture. But concentrations of Victoriana, and an occasional landmark, are to be found in western Alameda County. A little to the north, in Contra Costa County, John Muir's old home is worth a visit, as is the former state capital of Benicia—just across the bridge on I-680.

Benicia

Frisbie-Walsh House, c.1850. 235 East L. One of a trio of prefabricated Gothic cottages shipped 'round the Horn from New England during the gold rush era. Originally occupied by John and Epifanía Vallejo Frisbie, it was later purchased by John Walsh, a Nova Scotian sea captain who served as customs collector in Benicia in the early 1850s. Recently restored, it is now a bed and breakfast, *The Captain Walsh House.* 707-747-5653.

Martinez

John Muir National Historic Site, 1882. 4202 Alhambra. The Italianate residence of the naturalist-author. Open for tours. 510-228-8860.

Alameda

• Rivaling even San Francisco, Alameda has one of the finest and most concentrated selections of Victorian homes in the United States. The city, which occupies an island all its own, has representative examples of almost every Victorian style from Italianate to Shingle. *p. 42.*

Anthony House, 1876. 1630 Central. The former home of railroad official John Anthony is, by all accounts, the finest Italianate suburban townhouse in Alameda.

• **Brehaut House**, 1893. 2070 San Jose. Architect: C. H. Shaner. An oft-photographed Queen Anne based on a pattern-book design by the Knoxville mail-order architect George Franklin Barber. *p. 39.*

Jacobi House, 1890. 816 Grand. A shingled, corner-towered Queen Anne built for Louis H. Jacobi, treasurer of the local phone company.

Shingle Style House, c.1890. 1098 Sherman. A Shingle style residence that would be at home on the East Coast.

Oakland

Oakland's city hall has long encouraged its citizens' rehabilitation efforts. As a result the city has many well-preserved Victorian homes, especially on the east side, where several Newsom creations are still standing. There are also a number of interesting Victorians in and around the downtown area.

• **Camron-Stanford House**, 1876. 1418 Lakeside Dr. Italianate in style, the house is the last of the Victorian mansions on Lake Merritt. It originally belonged to Alice Camron—née Marsh—daughter of a wealthy cattleman. It was later acquired by Leland Stanford's brother, Josiah, and is now a house museum sponsored by the city. 510-836-1976. *p. 49.*

Queen Anne House, 1888. 1806 10th. Architects: S. & J. Newsom. A late Queen Anne residence with Classical Revival tendencies.

Paul House, 1894. 2035 East 10th. A shingled corner-towered Queen Anne.

Cottage, 1887. 2304 9th. Architects: S. & J. Newsom. A raised-basement, story-and-a-half cottage with canted bay and Eastlake touches.

William Henshaw House, c.1890. 544 E. 14th. A turreted Queen Anne similar to Los Angeles' *Hale House.*

Berkeley

Boudrow House, c.1893. 1536 Oxford. A corner-towered Queen Anne with Eastlake details.

Hayward Vicinity

Meek Estate, 1869. Hampton at Boston. The Italianate home of William Meek, an early champion of the California fruit industry. Tours by the Hayward Area Historical Society. 510-581-0223.

McConaghy House, c.1880s. 18701 Hesperian Blvd, San Lorenzo. Stick style Queen Anne. Tours: 510-581-0223.

The Peninsula

The extraordinary nineteenth-century homes that once belonged to San Francisco's neighbors to the south have mostly disappeared. Among the departed is one of the gaudiest residences ever built in California—*Linden Towers*—an immense, eclectic castle commissioned in 1878 by Virginia City bonanza king James Flood. Designed by Laver, Cutlett, and Lenzen it was painted blinding white and was popularly known as Flood's Wedding Cake. Too expensive to maintain in modern times, it was razed in 1934.

The Peninsula still harbors more than its share of millionaire abodes, but most of them are of later vintage. Nonetheless, scattered here and there are some interesting Victorian-era structures, including two fine Gothic Revival cottages.

Further south in San Jose, which has been the site of relentless development since World War II, the story is much the same. But the *Winchester House* and the San Jose Historical Museum are worth a look.

Redwood City

Benjamin Lathrop House, 1860. 627 Hamilton. A two-story Gothic Revival cottage complete with fancy gable trim. 415-365-5564.

Atherton

• **Captain Watkins House**, 1860. 25 Isabella. An expansive Gothic cottage that was prefabricated in Connecticut and shipped to California. *p. 11.*

Menlo Park

Southern Pacific Depot, c.1880. 1100 Merrill. Originally a train station in the Eastlake style, the building is now an office of the the local chamber of commerce.

Palo Alto

Queen Anne House, 1894. 706 Cowper. A villa with a wealth of spindlework.

San Jose

San Jose Historical Museum. 1600 Senter Rd. With nearly thirty relocated and restored structures, the SJHM is the largest Victorian park in the state. Buildings include nineteenth-century shops, offices, a hotel, and several houses. 408-287-2290.

Winchester House. 525 S. Winchester Blvd. According to the story, Mrs. Winchester, widow of the rifle maker, entertained the superstition that she would die when the house was completed. To thwart the reaper, she kept carpenters busy with improbable expansion schemes, a ploy that succeeded for several years. The front of the house is basically Queen Anne with Stick and Eastlake touches. Open for tours. 408-247-2000.

Queen Anne House, Alameda, c.1893

Victorian Duplex, Alameda, c.1895

"Seven Gables Inn," Pacific Grove, 1886

Lacy House, "Green Gables Inn," Pacific Grove, 1888

Gray House, Santa Cruz, 1891

The Central Coast

The long stretch of coast that separates Northern from Southern California is better known for its natural beauty than for its architecture. But some seaside communities that began as resorts in the nineteenth century retain some interesting Victoriana. The same is true of several agricultural towns in the coastal valleys north and south of the Los Padres Range.

Santa Cruz

Santa Cruz thrived as a vacation spot in the last quarter of the nineteenth century and has a fine collection of buildings from that era. Although many of its older commercial structures were damaged in the recent Loma Prieta quake, the Victorian residences seem to have survived nicely. Most were built by local "carpitects" who made up for a lack of formal training with a wealth of hands-on experience.

• **McPheters House**, 1882. 203 Highland. Architects: C. Graham & Son. A mansardic version of the gabled-ell cottage. Builder James Stewart McPheters constructed it as his own residence from a plan featured in Bicknell's *Detail, Cottage, and Constructive Architecture.* **p. 20.**

Eastlake House, c.1880. 207 Mission. An Italian Villa style residence with a square tower and Eastlake gables.

• **Gray House**, 1891. 250 Ocean View. Builder: Le Baron R. Olive. The Queen Anne residence of Captain W. W. Gray. Another, similar house on Ocean View seems also to have been built by Le Baron Olive. **p. 43.**

Queen Anne Row Houses, c.1890. NE corner Lincoln and Chestnut. A late nineteenth-century row house group, very unusual for a small town.

Watsonville

• **Judge Lee House**, 1894. 128 East Beach. Architect: William Henry Weeks. A sophisticated Shingle-Queen Anne cottage. Once the home of a local jurist, it is now used as an office building. **p. 63.**

• **Morris Tuttle Mansion**, 1899. 723 E. Lake. Architect: W. H. Weeks. This large, elaborate Free Classic Queen Anne was built for a prosperous Pajaro Valley farmer. It is now an office building. **p. 62.**

Salinas

• **Steinbeck House**, 1897. 132 Central. The boyhood home of the author of *The Grapes of Wrath, Cannery Row,* etc. Restored by the Valley Guild, it is now a shop and restaurant. Tour information: 408-424-2735. **p. 64.**

• **Sargent House**, 1896. 154 Central. Architect: W. H. Weeks. A Shingle style residence with broad overhanging gable and wave-form shingle patterning. Now an office building. **p. 65.**

• **Queen Anne Cottage**, 1898. 402 Cayuga. Queen Anne with a profusion of Eastlake decoration. **p. 55.**

Pacific Grove

Monterey may be famous for its early nineteenth-century adobes, but neighboring Pacific Grove has a range of architecture from the Victorian era. The town started out in 1875 as a Christian summer resort where Robert Louis Stevenson perceived "a life of teetotalism, religion, and flirtation, which I am willing to think blameless and agreeable." The earliest structures were summer vacation cottages, but more substantial homes soon appeared, some of which have found new life as restaurants, inns, and bed and breakfasts.

• **Lacy House**, 1888. 104 5th. A tudor-inflected Gothic house that was built and probably designed by William Lacy, an English engineer and architecture buff— reputedly for his mistress. It is now the *Green Gables Inn.* 408-375-2095. *p. 43.*

• **Stevinson House**, 1883. 129 Pacific. A Gothic Revival style vacation cottage built by a San Joaquin Valley rancher. *p. 11.*

Store Building, 1893. 541 Lighthouse. An Eastlake-detailed commercial building, beautifully restored. Now the *Victorian Corner Restaurant.*

• **Seven Gables Inn**, 1886. 550 Ocean View Blvd. Queen Anne style. 408-372-4341. *p. 43.*

Arroyo Grande

• **Pitkin House**, 1885. 789 Valley Rd. A square-towered villa with Stick and Eastlake details. Originally the home of rancher and developer Charles Pitkin, it is now *The Crystal Rose Inn.* 805-481-5566. *p. 21.*

San Luis Obispo

Jack House, 1876. 536 Marsh. A vintage Italianate residence now maintained by the city. The house and gardens are open for public tours. 805-781-7308.

The Central Valley

Technically it's the *Sacramento* in the north and the *San Joaquin* in the south, but to most people it's simply the "Big Valley." Whatever you call it, the four-hundred-mile vale that separates the Sierras from the coast ranges is one of the most productive agricultural areas in the United States. As might be expected, it is liberally strewn with late-nineteenth-century farmhouses, the residences of early settlers, some of whom arrived even before annexation. As exemplified by the General Bidwell mansion in Chico, the earliest tended to be Italianate in style; those of later vintage are generally Queen Anne derivatives.

A drive along old Highway 99 will reveal many interesting, but widely scattered examples. Almost every valley town founded before the turn of the century seems to have its own local monument.

Sacramento Valley

Red Bluff

In its early years the town prospered as a logging center at the head of navigation on the Sacramento River. A number of Victorian homes in a range of styles are preserved in the older neighborhood centered around Washington and Jefferson Streets.

• **Kelly-Griggs House**, c.1880. 311 Washington. The double-bayed Italianate residence of sheep rancher Sidney Allen Griggs. It is now a house museum open for public tours. 916-527-1129. *p. 49.*

Chico

Chico was originally the homestead of General John Bidwell who led the first party of American settlers across the Sierras. Besides his residence, the town has managed to retain some other interesting Victorians.

• **Bidwell Mansion**, 1867. 525 the Esplanade. Architect: Henry W. Cleaveland. Bidwell hired a well-known eastern architect to design this prototypical Italian villa. Now a State Historic Monument, it is located on the California State University campus. 916-895-6144. *p. 46.*

Bidwell Mansion, Chico, 1867

46

Gable Mansion, Woodland, 1885

Woodland

A few miles north of Sacramento, the small town of Woodland has a wonderful sampling of nineteenth-century architecture. The Queen Anne and Eastlake styles are well represented, and the Gothic Revival makes an appearance in the Callen-Rhodes House. But the town is especially rich in Italianate residences ranging from the Gable Mansion, an imposing villa, to suburban townhouses.

• **Gable Mansion**, 1885. 659 1st. A large bracketed Italian villa with Eastlake accretions. It was originally the home of a prosperous rancher. *p. 47.*

• **Queen Anne House**, c.1890. 638 1st. An Eastlake detailed Queen Anne featuring elaborate horseshoe and basket arches. *p. 54.*

• **Callen-Rhodes-Laugenour House**, 1873. 704 2nd. The lumber for this Gothic cottage was milled in Virginia from California redwood and shipped to Woodland for construction. Originally owned by William Callen, it was subsequently acquired by businessman John Milton Rhodes. In 1995 John and Pegee Laugenour completed the restoration begun by a former owner. *p. 11.*

• **Stephens-Ott House**, 1876. 708 College. Construction: A. & J. Stamp. Originally the home of a local banker, this two-story Italianate suburban house was enlarged in 1901. More recently Keith and Noreen Ott restored and painted it in period colors. *p. 49.*

Grafton-Barrow House, 1876. 640 College. A two-story, Italianate house similar to several of its neighbors.

Sacramento

The demands of progress, government, and freeways have tended to flatten historical architecture in the capital city, so many of its old houses have disappeared. Both the city and the state have tried to rectify this loss with such redevelopment projects as *Old Sacramento*.

• **Old Governor's Mansion**, 1874. 16th and H. Architect: Nathaniel D. Goodel. This elaborate Second Empire mansion, originally built for hardware merchant Albert Gallatin, served California's governors from 1903 until 1967. Open for public tours. 916-445-4209. *p. 20.*

Stanford-Lathrop House, c.1861. 802 N St. Architect: Seth Babson. A two-story Georgian house capped with a mansard roof. It was once the Sacramento residence of railroad baron and former governor Leland Stanford. Tour information: 916-324-0575.

Crocker Art Museum, 1872. 216 O St. Architect: Seth Babson. Sumptuous interiors house the oldest art museum in the west. 916-264-5423.

Golden State Museum. 1020 O St. Located in the California State Archives building, the museum opened in 1998 and features photographic and media displays of vintage California architecture. 916-653-7715.

Old Sacramento Historic District. 925 The Embarcadero. Wedged between Interstate 5 and the Sacramento River is this restored remnant of the city's original waterfront business district. Besides some interesting brick buildings, the district also features the state-sponsored railroad museum. 916-445-4209.

Stephens-Ott House, Woodland, 1876

Kelly-Griggs House, Red Bluff, c.1880

Parsons-Ochsner House, National City, c.1880

Camron-Stanford House, Oakland, 1876

49

W. S. Clark House, "An Elegant Victorian Mansion," Eureka, 1888

L. M. Smith House, Ferndale, 1894

Eastlake Storefront, Ferndale, 1896

G. W. Morse House, Eureka, 1893

Carter House Inn, Eureka, c.1980

Elizur Steele House, National City, c.1879

Phillips House, Los Angeles, 1887

Cross House, "The Old Victorian Inn," Stockton, 1890

Queen Anne House, Woodland, c.1890

Bushyhead House, San Diego, 1889

Queen Anne Cottage, Salinas, 1898

Sherman-Gilbert House, San Diego, 1889

Queen Anne House, Los Angeles, c.1890

Edwards Mansion, Redlands, 1890

Torrey House, Eureka, 1892

Weller House, Los Angeles, 1887

Goode House, Glendale, 1897

Queen Anne House, Pasadena, 1887

Bair-Stokes House, Arcata, 1888

Wright-Mooers House, Los Angeles, 1894

Pinney House, Sierra Madre, c.1888

Tuttle Mansion, Watsonville, 1899

Julius Lee House, Watsonville, 1894

Bettner "Heritage" House, Riverside, 1892

Steinbeck House, Salinas, 1897

Shingled Cottage, San Rafael, 1887

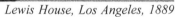

Lewis House, Los Angeles, 1889

Sessions House, Los Angeles, 1888

Sargent House, Salinas, 1896

San Joaquin Valley

Stockton

The old inland port city of Stockton has been malled and redeveloped, but the residential neighborhood north of the town center retains some nice Victorian homes, at least one of which is credited to the Newsom Brothers.

Newell House, c.1888. 1107 North San Joaquin. Queen Anne with Eastlake details: Attributed to S. & J. Newsom. Now used for business offices.

Swett House, 1883. 143 Acacia. Architects: S. & J. Newsom. Queen Anne with Eastlake details.

• **Cross House**, 1890. 207 Acacia. Former Queen Anne residence of Dr. Lester E. Cross. Now *The Old Victorian Inn.* 209-462-1613. *p. 54.*

Modesto

Oramil McHenry Mansion, c.1875. 906 15th. An imposing mansardic manse. Tour information: 209-577-5341.

Fresno

Meux Home Museum, 1889. 1000 R St. The Queen Anne residence of Thomas R. Meux, an early Fresno physician. Purchased by the city and restored by volunteer groups, it is now open to the public. 209-233-8007.

Kearney Mansion, 1903. 7160 W. Kearney Blvd. The frenchified Queen Anne residence of horticulturist Martin Theodore Kearney. The mansion is maintained and administered by the Fresno Historical Society and is open for tours. 209-441-0862.

The Mother Lode Country

Because mining towns were often constructed overnight and abandoned just as quickly, their buildings are generally of historical rather than architectural interest. The former boom town of Bodie on the eastern shoulder of the Sierras shows little trace of what we would recognize today as Victorian style: the overall feeling is one of "Wild West" gone to seed.

Ghost towns may be romantic, but the Mother Lode country also has dozens of gold towns that managed graceful transitions into the twentieth century. Nevada City, Placerville, Sonora, and Yreka are among those that retain some interesting Victorian remnants, in particular Gothic Revival churches.

Most of the former mining towns of the Sierra Nevada Mother Lode country are on or within easy shouting distance of Highway 49. The gold towns of Trinity and Shasta Counties—French Gulch, Shasta, Weaverville, and others—are clustered on or around Highway 299 near the Oregon border.

Mono County

Bodie

• Bodie's economy collapsed twenty years after its founding, when the gold that created it in the late 1870s began to run out. The townsfolk abandoned its 160 frame structures to the high desert and, ultimately, the state of California. The entire ghost town is now a State Historical Park. 619-647-6445. *p. 68.*

Bridgeport

• **Towle House**, 1878. Bridge at Hwy. 395. Carpenter: Peter Nye. The Gothic Revival home of Joshua W. Towle, a former state of Mainer who operated one of the lumber mills that supplied Bodie. Still in the family, it is the residence of some of Towle's descendants. *p. 10.*

Mono County Courthouse, 1880. A beautifully preserved, wood-frame courthouse in the Italianate style.

Highway 49

Nevada City

• **Queen Anne House**, c.1860-90. 441 Washington. Additions over the course of decades have turned an ordinary clapboard house into a corner-towered Queen Anne. It was recently renovated by restoration architect Greg Wolters for Gary and Lorrie Ericson. *p. 69.*

Marsh House, 1873. 254 Boulder. The Italianate home of a cabinet maker and lumber dealer who built several other homes in Nevada City.

Trinity Episcopal Church, 1854. Nevada at Grove. Another fine Gothic Revival church.

Fire House No. 1, c.1880. 214 Broad. A narrow fire station surmounted by a watchtower-pavilion.

Grass Valley

Cambell-Jones House, 1880. 328 S. Church. Originally the home of a local merchant, it was later used as a hospital. It is now the Swan-Levine House, a bed and breakfast. 916-272-1873.

Horan House, 1874. 415 Main. The original residence of miner James Horan has blossomed into a Queen Anne.

• **Emmanuel Episcopal Church**, 1854. Church St. near Walsh. The unpainted board-and-batten siding makes an eloquent statement befitting one of the oldest Gothic Revival churches in the state. *p. 68.*

Auburn

Placer County Courthouse, 1894. Architect: John M. Curtis. A neoclassical government building—domed, symmetrical, large, and imposing.

Methodist Church, 1858. Gothic Revival.

Placerville

Combellack-Blair House, 1895. 2059 Cedar Ravine. Queen Anne former residence of William Hill Combellack. Now a bed and breakfast. 916-622-3764.

San Andreas

Queen Anne House, 1895. 248 Charles. Restrained Queen Anne with a horseshoe-arched front window. Now *The Robin's Nest,* a bed and breakfast. 209-754-1076.

Columbia

The entire town is a State Historical Park, touristy but mostly authentic, with brick commercial buildings and churches dating from the late 1850s.

Sonora

• **St. James Episcopal Church**, 1859. Snell at Washington. A very fine board-and-batten Gothic Revival church. *p. 68.*

Frank A. Morgan House, 1888. Snell at Washington. A towered villa with Eastlake decoration. Its Stick style porch braces are more typical of the East than of the West Coast.

Methodist Church, Bodie, c.1876

St. James Episcopal, Sonora, 1859

Emmanuel Episcopal, Grass Valley, 1854

Queen Anne House, Nevada City, c.1860-90

Southern California

In the northern half of the state entire communities of venerable old buildings can still be found. In Southern California, the lives of Victorians are more tenuous and fugitive. But even in the fast lane there are small enclaves and scattered monuments that owe their continued existence to a combination of luck, benign neglect, and the efforts, sometimes heroic, of local preservationists.

Santa Barbara & Ventura

Santa Barbara

Though often identified with its Mission Revival architecture, Santa Barbara's oldest neighborhoods are filled with Victorian-era homes, some of them very interesting indeed.

Eberle House, 1892. 36 W. Valerio.. A restrained Queen Anne cottage. Now *The Cheshire Cat,* a bed and breakfast. 805-569-1610.

Edwards House, 1888. 1721 Santa Barbara. Architect: Thomas Nixon. Eastlake-Queen Anne.

The Parsonage, 1882. 1600 Olive. The Queen Anne style rectory of Trinity Episcopal Church. Now a bed and breakfast. 805-962-9336.

Baxter House, c. 1875. 302 W. Micheltorena. A French cottage with "Graham gables"—very rare in California.

Ventura

St. Johns Church, 1888. 896 East Main. Gothic Revival.

Los Angeles County

Los Angeles

Central L.A.

• **Stimson House**, 1891. 2421 S. Figueroa. Architect: Carroll H. Brown. A Romanesque structure of Arizona sandstone built for Chicago lumberman Thomas D. Stimson. Now a convent. *p. 73.*

Angelino Heights

This is one of the few neighborhoods in Los Angeles that has managed to retain a semblance of its original, nineteenth-century character. For most of this century its old homes languished in disrepair; but in the past few decades, energetic homeowners have brought a positive bloom back to the community. Carroll Avenue alone boasts at least a dozen nicely restored Victorians.

• **Phillips House**, 1887. 1300 Carroll. A large Queen Anne residence with a wealth of Eastlake details. *p. 54.*

• **Sessions House**, 1888. 1330 Carroll. Architect: Joseph C. Newsom. Queen Anne-Shingle style. *p. 65.*

• **Weller House**, c.1887. 824 Kensington. A Queen Anne residence that seems to be based on a pattern-book design by the mail-order architect G. F. Barber. *p. 57.*

McArthur Park

• **Lewis House**, 1889. 425 Miramar. Architect: Joseph C. Newsom. A Queen Anne-Shingle style residence. *p. 65.*

• **Wright-Mooers House**, 1894. 818 S. Bonnie Brae. Contractor: Frank L. Wright. The eclectic Queen Anne home of Frederick Mitchell Mooers, a former newspaper reporter who discovered the Yellow Aster Mine. *p. 60.*

Santa Monica

Angel's Attic, 1893. 516 Colorado. Recently restored, the oldest home in the city is now a museum featuring antique dollhouses, miniatures, and toys. 310-394 8331.

San Pedro

Point Fermin Lighthouse, 1874. Paseo del Mar near Pacific. A Stick style house topped with a tower and beacon. It was restored in the 1960s by the Sons and Daughters of the Golden West.

Glendale

• **Goode House**, 1897. 119 N. Cedar. The last Eastlake-Queen Anne residence in the city. Originally built by Edgar D. Goode, a Glendale civic activist, it was recently restored as the centerpiece of a twenty-five-unit housing complex for the disabled. *p. 58.*

Pasadena

Williams House, *Hillmont,* 1887. NW Corner Hill and Mountain. Architect: Harry Ridgeway. A large and sophisticated Queen Anne residence by Pasadena's first professional architect.

• **Queen Anne House**, 1887. 510 Locke Haven. Architects: Merihew & Ferris. The Eastlake details that adorn the facade and porch are striking, individual, and two cuts above average. *p. 59.*

Heritage Square

The Cultural Heritage Foundation of Southern California was so concerned about the future of some of the older structures in greater Los Angeles that it acquired a parcel of land in Highland Park to serve as a sanctuary for them. To date the foundation has rescued and relocated more than a half dozen nineteenth-century structures to this outdoor museum of Victoriana. 3800 Homer, (Ave 43 exit off the Pasadena Freeway.) 818-449-0193.

Hale House, 1888. Originally owned by real estate developer George Washburn Morgan, this Queen Anne flagship has been relocated, restored, and repainted in its original colors.

Shaw House, *Valley Knudsen Garden Residence,* c.1883. Carpenter: Richard Shaw. A French cottage designed and meticulously constructed by a Los Angeles cabinet maker.

Perry House, *Mount Pleasant,* 1876. Architect: Ezra F. Kyzor. A bracketed Italianate demi-mansion that displays most of the features associated with the style.

Arcadia

• **Lucky Baldwin House**, 1881. 301 N. Baldwin. Architect: A. A. Bennett. A Gothic-Queen Anne bungalow built as a guest house on the grounds of the E. J. Baldwin estate in Rancho Santa Anita, now part of the Los Angeles State and County Arboretum. 626-447-8207. *p. 72.*

Sierra Madre

• **Pinney House**, c.1888. 225 Lima. Architects: S. & J. Newsom with an assist from Hollywood. Originally a hotel, the structure acquired its oversized porch spindles and swans-neck pediment when it served as a movie set. *p. 61.*

City of Industry

Workman House, 1820-70. 15413 E. Don Julian Rd. A picturesque reworking by architect Ezra Kysor of the adobe-clad, frame structure erected by William Workman in the 1840s. It is now part of the city's *Workman-Temple Family Homestead Museum,* which features several other historical structures. 818-968-8492.

Lucky Baldwin House, Arcadia, 1881

Stimson House, Los Angeles, 1891

Monrovia

Queen Anne House, c.1890. 150 N. Myrtle. A substantial Queen Anne with Eastlake details.

Queen Anne House, c.1887. 225 Monroe. The Queen Anne home of Monrovia's founder.

Queen Anne House, c.1887. 250 N. Primrose. A large and nicely maintained Queen Anne residence.

Orange & Riverside Counties

Orange

There are quite a few Free Classic Queen Anne homes scattered around the City of Orange. But its most distinctive feature is a well-preserved town square (Glassell at Chapman) that would be at home in the Midwest.

Santa Ana

Discovery Museum, c.1900. 3101 West Harvard. A late Queen Anne farmhouse open for tours by the public. 714-540-0404.

Howe Waffle House, 1889. 120 Civic Center Drive. The Queen Anne home of Willella Howe, Santa Ana's first woman doctor, who delivered more than a thousand babies. Relocated, restored, and maintained by the Santa Ana Historical Preservation Society, it is open for tours by appointment. 714-547-9645.

El Toro

Heritage Hill Historical Park, c.1890s. 25151 Serrano Rd. The park comprises four historical Orange County structures, including a church and schoolhouse. Open for tours. 714-855-2028.

Riverside

• **Bettner House**, 1892. 8193 Magnolia. Architect: John Walls. The sophisticated Queen Anne-Shingle style residence of Catherine Bettner, widow of a wealthy orange grower, was restored by the Riverside Museum Associates some years back. It is now *The Riverside Heritage House,* a museum open for tours. 909-689-1333. ***p. 64.***

Redlands

Perhaps because its larger neighbors Riverside and San Bernardino absorbed the brunt of modern development in the area, Redlands has been able to retain a nice selection of nineteenth-century residences, including the famous Morey Mansion.

Kimberly Crest House, 1897. 1325 Prospect Dr. The exceptional, towered, Chateauesque residence of the Kimberlys of Kimberly-Clark fame. The house and gardens are open for tours by the public on Thursdays and Sunday afternoons. 909-792-2111.

• **Morey Mansion**, 1890. 190 Terracina. Writer John Maas dubbed this elaborate Queen Anne Villa "America's favorite Victorian." It was designed and contructed by ship builder David Morey. It is now the *Morey Mansion Bed & Breakfast.* 909-793-7970. ***p. 7.***

• **Edwards Mansion**, 1890. 2064 Orange Tree Lane. Originally the home of citrus grower James Edwards, this spindlework Queen Anne house was moved to its present site in 1973. Restored by Donald Wilcott, it is now used as a reception hall for weddings, business lunches, etc. 909-793-2031. ***p. 56.***

Hoag House, 1888. 816 High. Queen Anne home of Isaac Newton Hoag and his wife Georgianna.

San Diego County

Carlsbad

Neiman's, 1888. Carlsbad Blvd. at Carlsbad Village Dr. An enormous Queen Anne inn plentifully decorated with Stick style and Eastlake details. It is now a restaurant.

Santa Fe Railroad Depot. Carlsbad Blvd. at Carlsbad Village Dr. A Stick style railroad depot now in use by the local chamber of commerce.

San Diego

Heritage Park

• Juan and Harney Streets, adjacent to Old Town. Initiated by the Save Our Heritage Organization and maintained by the county, Heritage Park shelters a half dozen restored and relocated Victorian structures. *p. 80.*

• **Sherman-Gilbert House**, 1889. Architects: Comstock & Trotsche. An eccentric, Stick style residence dating from San Diego's first boom period. Now a shop. *p. 55.*

• **Bushyhead House**, 1889. The Stick style home of Cherokee newspaper editor Edward Bushyhead. *p. 55.*

Christian House, 1889. A shingled, corner-towered Queen Anne. Now the *Heritage Park B & B.* 619-299-6832.

Temple Beth Israel, 1889. Classical Revival. The second oldest synagogue in the west. Now a community center.

Downtown

• **Long-Waterman House**, 1889. 2408 1st. Architect: D. B. Benson. A sophisticated Queen Anne Villa. Now an office building. *p. 76.*

• **Shepherd House**, *Villa Montezuma*, 1887. 1925 K. An elaborate and eclectic residence with Moorish touches and sumptuous interiors. Built by the city to lure author-musician Jesse Shepherd to town, it is now a house museum. 619-239-2211. *Back Cover.*

William Heath Davis House, c.1850s. 410 Island. A prefabricated salt box shipped from New England. It is now the headquarters of the Gaslamp Quarter Foundation.

Coronado

Coronado Victorian House, 1894. 1000 8th. A bed and breakfast that also offers dance lessons—a ploy to bypass city restrictions on B and B's. 618-435-2200.

Hotel Del Coronado, 1888. 1500 Orange. Architects: James & Merritt Reid. This grand and legendary Victorian hotel on the eastern shore of the vast Pacific is one of the last of the breed. 800-HOTELDEL.

National City

An attempt in the late 1880s to make National City the leading community on the San Diego Bay came to naught. As a result, many of the town's vintage homes are still standing today.

George Kimball House, 1887. 1515 L. An Italianate box built by one of the brothers who developed National City in the 1880s.

• **Elizur Steele House**, c.1879. 904 8th. Stick style—more or less—with a square tower. *p. 54.*

• **Parsons-Ochsner House**, c.1880. 437 G. Another of the Italianate residences built during National City's heyday. *p. 49.*

• **Dickenson-Boal House**, c.1887. 1433 E. 24th. Architects: Comstock & Trotsche. A large, corner-towered Queen Anne villa with Eastlake details. It was recently renovated by developer Jim Ladd. *p. 77.*

Long-Waterman House, San Diego, 1889

Dickenson-Boal House, National City, c.1887

Select Bibliography

Andrews, Wayne. *American Gothic: Its Origins, Its Trials, Its Triumphs.* New York: Random House, 1975.

Architectural Resources Group. *Eureka: An Architectural View.* Eureka Heritage Society, Inc., 1987.

Bear, Dorothy and Beth Stebbins. *Mendocino.* Mendocino Historical Research, 1973.

Brammer, Alex (ed.) *Victorian Classics of San Francisco.* (A reprint of *Artistic Homes of California,* 1888) Sausalito: Windgate Press, 1987.

Bruegmann, Robert. *Benicia: Portrait of an Early California Town.* San Francisco: 101 Productions, 1980.

Cassese, Ellie. *A Tour of Nevada City Victorians.* Nevada City: By the author, 1982.

Chase, John. *The Sidewalk Companion to Santa Cruz Architecture.* Santa Cruz Historical Society, 1975.

Downing, Andrew Jackson. *The Architecture of Country Houses.* D. Appleton & Co, 1850. Reprint. Introduction by J. Stewart Johnson. New York: Dover, 1969.

Ferndale Museum. *The Victorian Homes of Ferndale.* Ferndale Museum, 1985.

Foley, Mary Mix. *The American House.* New York: Harper & Row, 1980.

Gebhard, David and Robert Winter. *A Guide to Architecture in Los Angeles & Southern California.* Salt Lake City: Peregrine Smith, 1977.

Gebhard, David, et al. *A Guide to Architecture in San Francisco & Northern California.* Salt Lake City: Peregrine Smith, 1976.

Gebhard, David, et al. *Samuel and Joseph Cather Newson: Victorian Architectural Imagery.* Santa Barbara: UCSB Art Museum, 1979.

Gottfried, Herbert and Jan Jennings, *American Vernacular Design: 1870-1940.* New York: Van Nostrand Reinhold, 1985.

Lewis, Betty, *W. H. Weeks, Architect.* Fresno: Panorama West, 1985.

Maas, John. *The Gingerbread Age.* New York: Bramhall House, 1952.

Newsom, Joseph C. and Samuel. *Picturesque California Homes,* San Francisco, 1884. Reprint. Los Angeles: Hennessey & Ingalls, 1978.

Kirker, Harold. *California's Architectural Frontier.* Salt Lake City: Peregrine Smith, 1986.

McAlester, Virginia and Lee. *A Field Guide to American Houses.* New York: Alfred E. Knopf, 1985.

Richey, Elinor. *The Ultimate Victorians of the Continental Side of San Francisco Bay.* Berkeley: Howell-North, 1970.

Van Kirk, Susie. *Reflections on Arcata's History: Eighty Years of Architecture.* City of Arcata, 1979.

Olmsted, Roger and T. H Watkins with photographs by Morley Baer. *Here Today, San Francisco's Architectural Heritage.* San Francisco: Chronicle, 1968.

About the Author

Kenneth Naversen is a photographer and writer who specializes in architectural and travel subjects. He has a masters degree in art history and photography and is a former recipient of an Art Critics Fellowship Grant from the National Endowment for the Arts. His photographic work has appeared in many regional and national publications; his writing credits include two previous books on vintage architecture: *West Coast Victorians: A Nineteenth-Century Legacy*; and *East Coast Victorians: Castles and Cottages.*

Heritage Park, San Diego